Made in the USA
Monee, IL
28 July 2021

74492077R00070